TAE KWON DO PATTERNS

CHON JI - DAN GUN - DO SAN

KTP Promotions

Introduction
This publication is intended to give students studying I.T.F Tae Kwon Do a comprehensive guide to patterns required to obtain yellow, green tag & green belt. It is not intended to replace regular training with a qualified instructor in a dojang. We hope this book will make the learning of patterns and associated Korean terminology easier and become an invaluable reference manual for all students of Tae Kwon Do.

ISBN 978-0-9560652-5-4

Disclaimer
Whilst every effort has been made to ensure that the content of this book is as technically accurate as possible, neither the authors nor the publishers can accept responsibility for any injury or loss sustained as a result of the use of this material. Reference to target areas and technique applications are intended as examples and not a definitive answer. The are many interpretations of techniques and this book is unable to highlight all possible applications or target areas.

Acknowledgments
Photographs: Sylvio Dokov Lifestyle Photography
Photo Editing: Dave Barson
Thank You to Master Terry Read 6th Dan & Master Miles Lutwyche 6th Dan
Editing: Keith O'Neill 5th Dan, Terry Read 6th Dan & Liz Read 5th Dan.
Design & Typeset: Paul Harding 5th Dan.

For more information about this publication contact:
www.taekwondo-books.com

First Published 2018

Published by KTP Promotions

Contents

Movement & Motion

Turning - Dolgi

The act of turning in Tae Kwon Do is built around 3 principles:
1. The ball of the foot is used as the pivot.
2. The heel is not lifted more than necessary to complete a smooth turn.
3. The duration of the turn should be as short as possible.

Stepping - Omgyo Didigi

Stepping is used to cover long distances. Stepping is broken down into single stepping (Ilbo Omgyo Didigi) and double stepping (Ibo Omgyo Didigi)

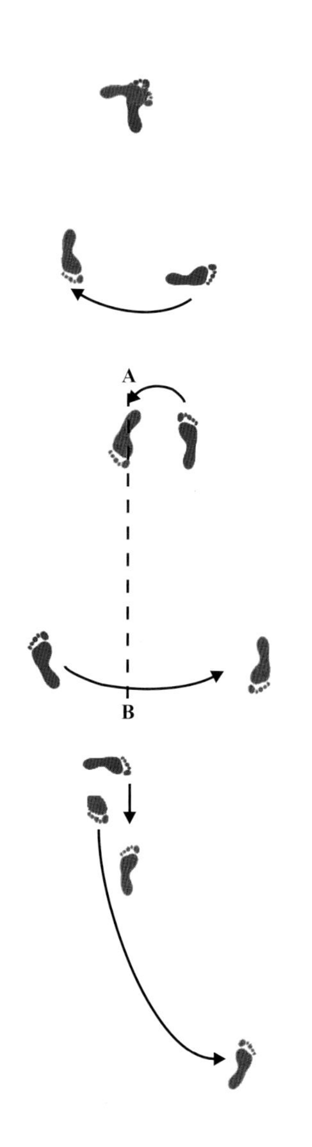

Step Turn - Omgyo Didimyo Dolgi

Step turning gives you the ability to face an opponent in any direction while being able to change direction and body position instantly. Step turns can also be used in any combination of sliding and shifting.

Spot Turn - Gujari Dolgi

A spot turn is used to turn 180 degrees and is performed by placing the front foot along the line (AB) and then the rear foot across to maintain the correct dimensions of the stance. Spot turning can be used for both defensive and attacking techniques.

Double Step Turn - Ibo Omgyo Didimyo Dolgi

Double step turning allows you to cover distance and change of direction. Although in theory any direction change is possible, it is mostly used in forward and backward movements.

Movement & Motion

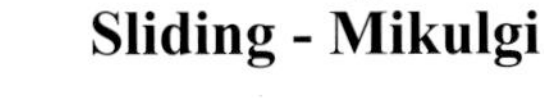

Sliding - Mikulgi

Sliding is highly effective for covering long distances in one fluid movement. Sliding motion can be combined with stepping and shifting.

Foot Shifting - Jajunbal

Foot shifting is used to cover short distances and is performed with either one or both feet. Foot shifting should be smooth without dragging or lifting the feet any more than necessary.

Slow Motion - Nurin Sokdo

Slow motion is used solely in patterns to demonstrate the theory of power, the element of speed being the only element omitted. Still one breath in and out per technique.

Fast Motion - Pparun Sokdo

Fast motion is used when combining several techniques without pausing, but in this type of motion the one breath in is exhaled proportionally between the techniques.

Normal Motion - Potong Sokdo

Normal motion requires a breath in followed by a breath out at the end of the technique, with a slight pause before the next technique.

Continuous Motion - Kesok Sokdo

Continuous motion is used when combining several techniques without pausing. Still one breath in and out per technique.

Connecting Motion - Honap Sokdo

Connecting motion is used when a no tension on impact technique is connected to a tension on impact technique. For example: Yul Gok - inhale on the hooking blocks, exhale on the punch.

About this book

This book contains 6 ways to reference your patterns. There is no substitution for training in a dojang with a qualified instructor, but this book provides an invaluable reference when solo training or revising for a grading.

Text
A detailed description of each technique, including the movement, direction and section of the body. Simple, concise and consistent.

Terminology
English and Korean terminology for every stance and technique is laid out clearly. The hand or foot part used is indicated and also example target areas.

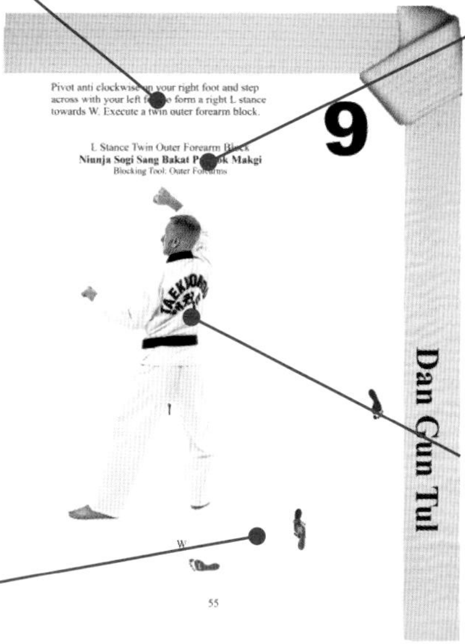

Full Colour Photographs
Each technique is supported by a full colour photograph and if necessary an inset photograph showing either the reverse angle of each movement or close up detail.

Foot Movement Plan
Each technique also contains a foot movement plan, together with directions to show where your feet were and where your feet should be on the current move. See page 5 for more details.

Step by Step

This book includes a step by step movement plan, which has smaller pictures spread over two pages for every 6 to 8 moves, to allow you to follow the pattern without any distraction.

New Techniques & Applications

This book highlights new techniques and the possible application which appear in each pattern. A full explanation of why techniques are performed is given, along with key areas to look out for.

How to use this book

This manual is designed to be used in conjunction with regular weekly training with a qualified instructor. The photographs, diagrams and wording are intended to be used as an aid to training and not a replacement.

This manual has been produced using foot movement diagrams (see below).

The directions N, S, E and W, relate to North, South, East and West. All patterns in this book begin facing south. See pages 133, 135, 137, 139 for cutouts to help with your patterns.

The **BLUE** foot shows your foot position from the previous move.
The **RED** foot shows the new position for the current move.

Examples

Walking Stance to Walking Stance
Double Stepping

N

L

R

L

R

S

Walking Stance to L Stance
Step Turn

Tae Kwon Do patterns

The following points should be considered when performing patterns:-

1. Patterns should begin and end on the same spot.
   This will indicate the performers accuracy.
2. Correct posture and facing must be maintained at all times.
3. Muscles of the body should be tensed or relaxed at the appropriate moments in the exercise.
4. The exercise should be performed in a rhythmic movement with absence of stiffness.
5. Each pattern should be accelerated or decelerated according to instructions.
6. Each pattern should be perfected before moving on to the next.
7. Students should know the purpose of each movement.
8. Students should perform each movement with realism.

Why do we kihap?

Correct breath control will not only improve ones stamina and speed, but will also focus the power of a technique. Correct breathing in martial arts is performed using the diaphragm. A sharp exhaling of breath during movement, with a sudden stop on impact of technique tenses the abdomen and maximises power and effort of delivery. The breathing technique used in Tae Kwon Do is called kihap or shout. Although called a shout, be careful not to use the vocal cords instead of the diaphragm, otherwise all the benefits will be lost.

Tae Kwon Do patterns

What is a pattern?

A set of fundamental movements, mainly defence and attack, set in a logical sequence against one or more imaginary opponents.

Why do we perform patterns?

To learn sparring techniques, stances, correct facing, improve facing, improve posture, focus movements, body shifting, breath control, muscle toning, learn to relax and tense muscles at the correct time and practice other techniques that are not possible in other areas of training.

Why do we learn the interpretations of patterns?

Pattern interpretations are derived from people and events in Korean history and show one or more of the tenets to give us inspiration.

Why are there 24 patterns?

The reason there are 24 patterns in Tae Kwon Do is because the founder, Major General Choi Hong Hi, compared the life of a man with a day in the life of the Earth, and believed that some people should strive to bequeath a good spiritual legacy to coming generations and in doing so gain immortality. Therefore, if we can leave something behind for the welfare of mankind, maybe it will be the most important thing to happen in our lives.

"Here I leave Tae Kwon Do for mankind.
As a trace of a man of the late 20th century
The 24 patterns, one day or all of my life".

Gen Choi Hong Hi
1918 - 2002

The Meaning of Chon Ji

Chon Ji means literally “Heaven and Earth”. In the Orient it is interpreted as the creation of the world, or the beginning of human history. Therefore, it is the initial pattern performed by the beginner. This pattern consists of two similar parts, one to represent Heaven and the other the Earth.

This pattern has 19 moves.

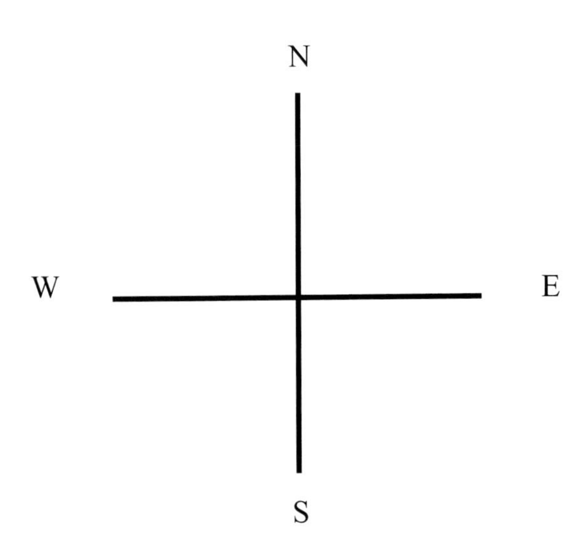

Movement Plan

In Depth Knowledge

Chon Ji

Chon Ji, or the "heavenly" lake, is the name of a large crater lake high in the Paektu Mountains. The crater is actually the top of an extinct volcano that is said to have been the first home of the legendary founder of Korea, Dan Gun. This is said by many to be the reason why Chon Ji is appropriately named because creation is the beginning of all things and this pattern establishes a good foundation for all the remaining patterns.

Chon Ji consists of two similar parts - one part representing Heaven - one part representing Earth. The stances and techniques in this pattern are the basic movements required for mastering all of the 24 patterns.

Begin in a parallel ready stance towards S.

Parallel Ready Stance
Narani Junbi Sogi

S

Pivot anti clockwise on your right foot and step forward with your left foot to form a left walking stance towards E. Execute a low block with your left outer forearm.

1

Walking Stance Outer Forearm Low Block
Gunnun Sogi Bakat Palmok Najunde Makgi
Blocking Tool: Outer Forearm

L

E

Chon Ji Tul

2

Step forward with your right foot to form a right walking stance towards E. Execute a middle obverse punch with your right fist.

Walking Stance Middle Obverse Punch
Gunnun Sogi Kaunde Baro Jirugi
Strike Tool: Fore Fist
Target Area: Solar Plexus

E

Pivot clockwise on your left foot and step forward with your right foot to form a right walking stance towards W. Execute a low block with your right outer forearm.

3

Walking Stance Outer Forearm Low Block
Gunnun Sogi Bakat Palmok Najunde Makgi
Blocking Tool: Outer Forearm

W

4

Step forward with your left foot to form a left walking stance towards W. Execute a middle obverse punch with your left fist.

Walking Stance Middle Obverse Punch
Gunnun Sogi Kaunde Baro Jirugi
Strike Tool: Fore Fist
Target Area: Solar Plexus

W

Pivot anti clockwise on your right foot and step across with your left foot to form a left walking stance towards S. Execute a low block with your left outer forearm.

5

Walking Stance Outer Forearm Low Block
Gunnun Sogi Bakat Palmok Najunde Makgi
Blocking Tool: Outer Forearm

S

6

Step forward with your right foot to form a right walking stance towards S. Execute a middle obverse punch with your right fist.

Walking Stance Middle Obverse Punch
Gunnun Sogi Kaunde Baro Jirugi
Strike Tool: Fore Fist
Target Area: Solar Plexus

L

S

Pivot clockwise on your left foot and step forward with your right foot to form a right walking stance towards N. Execute a low block with your right outer forearm.

Walking Stance Outer Forearm Low Block
Gunnun Sogi Bakat Palmok Najunde Makgi
Blocking Tool: Outer Forearm

N

R

L

8

Step forward with your left foot to form a left walking stance towards N. Execute a middle obverse punch with your left fist.

Walking Stance Middle Obverse Punch
Gunnun Sogi Kaunde Baro Jirugi
Strike Tool: Fore Fist
Target Area: Solar Plexus

Pivot anti clockwise on your right foot and step across with your left foot to form a right L stance towards W. Execute a middle block with your left inner forearm.

9

L Stance Inner Forearm Middle Block
Niunja Sogi An Palmok Kaunde Makgi
Blocking Tool: Inner Forearm

W

10

Step forward with your right foot to form a right walking stance towards W. Execute a middle obverse punch with your right fist.

Walking Stance Middle Obverse Punch
Gunnun Sogi Kaunde Baro Jirugi
Strike Tool: Fore Fist
Target Area: Solar Plexus

W

Pivot clockwise on your left foot and step across with your right foot to form a left L stance towards E. Execute a middle block with your right inner forearm.

11

L Stance Inner Forearm Middle Block
Niunja Sogi An Palmok Kaunde Makgi
Blocking Tool: Inner Forearm

E

R

12

Step forward with your left foot to form a left walking stance towards E. Execute a middle obverse punch with your left fist.

Walking Stance Middle Obverse Punch
Gunnun Sogi Kaunde Baro Jirugi
Strike Tool: Fore Fist
Target Area: Solar Plexus

L

E

Pivot anti clockwise on your right foot and step across with your left foot to form a right L stance towards N. Execute a middle block with your left inner forearm.

13

L Stance Inner Forearm Middle Block
Niunja Sogi An Palmok Kaunde Makgi
Blocking Tool: Inner Forearm

N

L

R

14

Step forward with your right foot to form a right walking stance towards N. Execute a middle obverse punch with your right fist.

Walking Stance Middle Obverse Punch
Gunnun Sogi Kaunde Baro Jirugi
Strike Tool: Fore Fist
Target Area: Solar Plexus

N

Chon Ji Tul

Pivot anti clockwise on your left foot and step across with your right foot to form a left L stance towards S. Execute a middle block with your right inner forearm.

15

L Stance Inner Forearm Middle Block
Niunja Sogi An Palmok Kaunde Makgi
Blocking Tool: Inner Forearm

L

R

S

Chon Ji Tul

16

Step forward with your left foot to form a left walking stance towards S. Execute a middle obverse punch with your left fist.

Walking Stance Middle Obverse Punch
Gunnun Sogi Kaunde Baro Jirugi
Strike Tool: Fore Fist
Target Area: Solar Plexus

S

Step forward with your right foot to form a right walking stance towards S. Execute a middle obverse punch with your right fist.

17

Walking Stance Middle Obverse Punch
Gunnun Sogi Kaunde Baro Jirugi
Strike Tool: Fore Fist
Target Area: Solar Plexus

L

S

18

Step backward with your right foot to form a left walking stance towards S. Execute a middle obverse punch with your left fist.

Walking Stance Middle Obverse Punch
Gunnun Sogi Kaunde Baro Jirugi
Strike Tool: Fore Fist
Target Area: Solar Plexus

S

Step backward with your left foot to form a right walking stance towards S. Execute a middle obverse punch with your right fist. Kihap to finish.

19

Walking Stance Middle Obverse Punch
Gunnun Sogi Kaunde Baro Jirugi
Strike Tool: Fore Fist
Target Area: Solar Plexus

L

R

S

End

Step forward with your left foot to form a parallel ready stance towards S.

Parallel Ready Stance
Narani Junbi Sogi

S

Generation of Power

Reaction Force
Pulling the opposite arm back in co-ordination with the strike creates a reaction force.
Concentration
Applying impact force onto the smallest target area.
Equilibrium
Use reaction arm for dynamic stability to keep the body balanced.
Breath Control
Tense abdomen to breathe out on impact.
Mass
Use hip twist and knee spring to increase body weight.
Speed
The most essential factor for power, however all the above factors contribute to speed.

New Techniques

Walking Stance
Gunnun Sogi

Walking stance is a strong training stance used to perform both attacking and defensive techniques. Your body weight is distributed evenly between your front and rear feet. The wide footprint makes this a very stable stance. The toes of your front foot face forward whilst your rear foot is angled at approximately 25 degrees outwards. A right walking stance is indicated by the right foot at the front and vice versa for a left walking stance.

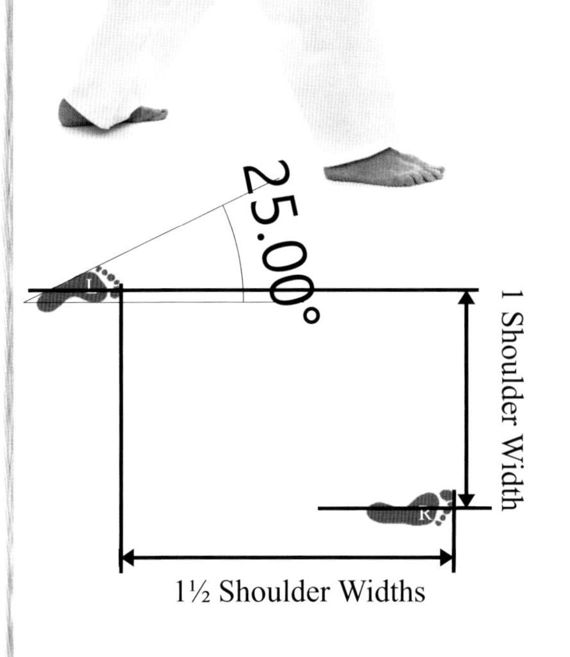

Weight Distribution
Rear 50%
Front 50%

Chon Ji Tul

New Techniques

L Stance
Niunja Sogi

L stance is used in both attacking and defensive techniques. The weight distribution allows your front foot to be easily deployed to kick an opponent. A right L stance is when your right leg is to the rear and bears the majority of your weight and vice versa for a left L stance. There is approximately a 2.5 cm gap between your heels to aid balance.

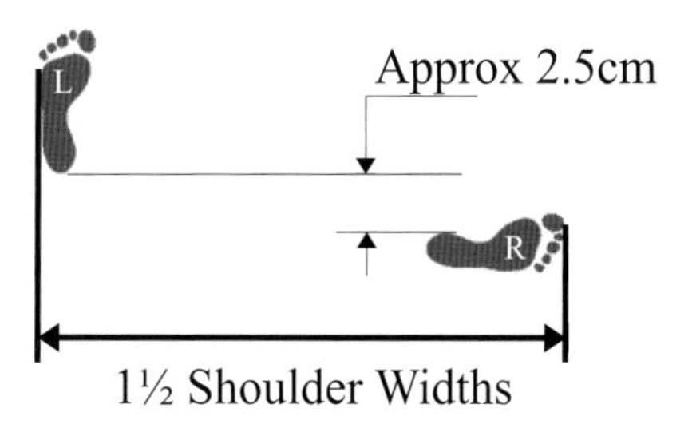

Weight Distribution
Rear 70%
Front 30%

New Techniques

Outer Forearm Low Block
Bakat Palmok Najunde Makgi

Chamber Postition

Outer forearm low block is used to defend against an opponent targeting your lower abdomen or groin. The block travels in an arc from the chamber position to finish inline with your front knee.

Application of Techniques

Like many blocks in Tae Kwon Do, this block is designed not only to deflect your opponents technique but also to smash or destroy the attacking tool. In this example the blocking arm would break or rupture the ankle joint/achilles tendon, thus immobilising your opponent and prevent further attack.

New Techniques

Inner Forearm Middle Block
An Palmok Kaunde Makgi

Middle block is used to defend against an attack aimed towards your solar plexus. Knuckles of your blocking arm finish inline with your lead shoulder at a 90 degree angle. This is a side facing block.

Chamber Position

Application of Techniques

This block can be used to defend against both hand and foot techniques. When performing this block ensure your blocking arm finishes inline with your shoulder and should not extend past the natural finish point.

1

Parallel Ready Stance

Walking Stance
Outer Forearm
Low Block

4

Walking Stance
Middle Obverse Punch

5

Walking Stance
Outer Forearm
Low Block

2

Walking Stance
Middle Obverse Punch

3

Walking Stance
Outer Forearm
Low Block

6

Walking Stance
Middle Obverse Punch

7

Walking Stance
Outer Forearm
Low Block

8

Walking Stance
Middle Obverse Punch

9

L Stance
Inner Forearm
Middle Block

12

Walking Stance
Middle Obverse Punch

13

L Stance
Inner Forearm
Middle Block

10

Walking Stance
Middle Obverse Punch

11

L Stance
Inner Forearm
Middle Block

14

Walking Stance
Middle Obverse Punch

15

L Stance
Inner Forearm
Middle Block

16

Walking Stance
Middle Obverse Punch

17

Walking Stance
Middle Obverse Punch

End

Parallel Ready Stance

18

Walking Stance
Middle Obverse Punch

19

Walking Stance
Middle Obverse Punch

The Meaning of Dan Gun

Dan Gun is named after the holy Dan Gun the legendary founder of Korea who established the country in 2333BC.

This pattern has 21 moves.

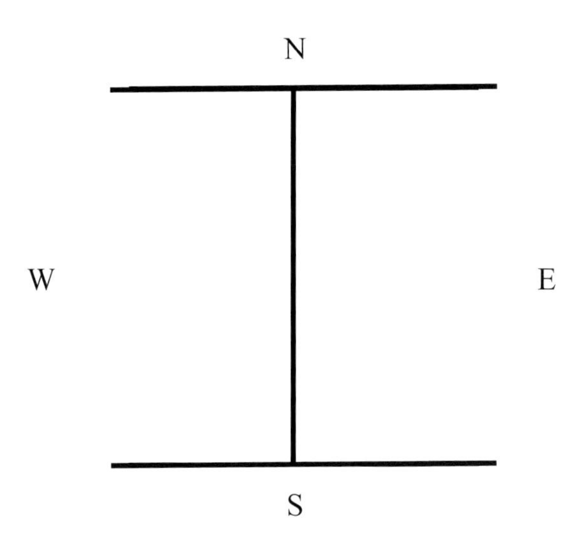

Movement Plan

Dan Gun

The Legend of Dan Gun

The "Lord of Heaven" Hwanin had a son, Hwanung, who yearned to live on he earth among the valleys and the mountains. His wish was granted and he lescended from Heaven to the Baekdu Mountain and founded the city of Sinsi (City of God). Along with his ministers of clouds, rain and wind, he nstituted laws and moral codes and taught humans various arts, medicine nd agriculture.

A tiger and a bear prayed to Hwanung that they may become human. Upon earing their prayers Hwanung gave them 20 cloves of garlic and a bundle of nugwort, ordering them to eat only this sacred food and remain out of the unlight for 100 days. The tiger gave up after about twenty days and left the ave. However, the bear remained and was transformed into a woman. Hwanung took her for his wife and soon she gave birth to a son, who was amed Dan Gun Wanggeom.

Dan Gun Wanggeom went on to become the legendary founder of Gojoseon, he first Korean kingdom in 2333 BC. It is thought to be located around resent day regions of Liaoning, Manchuria and the Korean Peninsula. Dan Gun is said to have lived to the ge of 1908 years old when he became a mountain God.

Although the term Dan Gun commonly refers to the ounder, some believe it was a title meaning "high riest" used by all rulers of Gojoseon and that Wanggeom was the proper name of the founder.

is said that all the punches in Dan Gun tul are high ection to symbolise Dan Gun scaling a mountain on his ay to becoming a God.

Dan Gun Wanggeom

Begin in a parallel ready stance towards S.

Parallel Ready Stance
Narani Junbi Sogi

Step across with your left foot to form a right L stance towards E. Execute a middle knife hand guarding block.

1

L Stance Knife Hand Middle Guarding Block
Niunja Sogi Sonkal Kaunde Daebi Makgi
Blocking Tool: Knife Hand

L

R E

2

Step forward with your right foot to form a right walking stance towards E. Execute a high obverse punch with your right fist.

Walking Stance High Obverse Punch
Gunnun Sogi Nopunde Baro Jirugi
Strike Tool: Fore Fist
Target Area: Nose

L

E

Pivot clockwise on your left foot and step across with your right foot to form a left L stance towards W. Execute a middle knife hand guarding block.

L Stance Knife Hand Middle Guarding Block
Niunja Sogi Sonkal Kaunde Daebi Makgi
Blocking Tool: Knife Hand

W

4

Step forward with your left foot to form a left walking stance towards W. Execute a high obverse punch with your left fist.

Walking Stance High Obverse Punch
Gunnun Sogi Nopunde Baro Jirugi
Strike Tool: Fore Fist
Target Area: Nose

W

Pivot anti clockwise on your right foot and step across with your left foot to form a left walking stance towards S. Execute a low block with your left outer forearm.

5

Walking Stance Outer Forearm Low Block
Gunnun Sogi Bakat Palmok Najunde Makgi
Blocking Tool: Outer Forearm

S

6

Step forward with your right foot to form a right walking stance towards S. Execute a high obverse punch with your right fist.

Walking Stance High Obverse Punch
Gunnun Sogi Nopunde Baro Jirugi
Strike Tool: Fore Fist
Target Area: Nose

L

R

S

Step forward with your left foot to form a left walking stance towards S. Execute a high obverse punch with your left fist.

7

Walking Stance High Obverse Punch
Gunnun Sogi Nopunde Baro Jirugi
Strike Tool: Fore Fist
Target Area: Nose

R

L

S

8

Step forward with your right foot to form a right walking stance towards S. Execute a high obverse punch with your right fist.

Walking Stance High Obverse Punch
Gunnun Sogi Nopunde Baro Jirugi
Strike Tool: Fore Fist
Target Area: Nose

L

R

S

Pivot anti clockwise on your right foot and step across with your left foot to form a right L stance towards W. Execute a twin outer forearm block.

9

L Stance Twin Outer Forearm Block
Niunja Sogi Sang Bakat Palmok Makgi
Blocking Tool: Outer Forearms

W

L

R

Dan Gun Tul

10

Step forward with your right foot to form a right walking stance towards W. Execute a high obverse punch with your right fist.

Walking Stance High Obverse Punch
Gunnun Sogi Nopunde Baro Jirugi
Strike Tool: Fore Fist
Target Area: Nose

W

Pivot clockwise on your left foot and step across with your right foot to form a left L stance towards E. Execute a twin outer forearm block.

11

L Stance Twin Outer Forearm Block
Niunja Sogi Sang Bakat Palmok Makgi
Blocking Tool: Outer Forearms

E

12

Step forward with your left foot to form a left walking stance towards E. Execute a high obverse punch with your left fist.

Walking Stance High Obverse Punch
Gunnun Sogi Nopunde Baro Jirugi
Strike Tool: Fore Fist
Target Area: Nose

E

Pivot anti clockwise on your right foot and step across with your left foot to form a left walking stance towards N. Execute a low block with your left outer forearm.

13

Walking Stance Outer Forearm Low Block
Gunnun Sogi Bakat Palmok Najunde Makgi
Blocking Tool: Outer Forearm

N

14

Remain in a walking stance towards N. Execute a rising block with your left outer forearm.

Walking Stance Outer Forearm Rising Block
Gunnun Sogi Bakat Palmok Chookyo Makgi
Blocking Tool: Outer Forearm

N

Step forward with your right foot to form a right walking stance towards N. Execute a rising block with your right outer forearm.

Walking Stance Outer Forearm Rising Block
Gunnun Sogi Bakat Palmok Chookyo Makgi
Blocking Tool: Outer Forearm

N

16

Step forward with your left foot to form a left walking stance towards N. Execute a rising block with your left outer forearm.

Walking Stance Outer Forearm Rising Block
Gunnun Sogi Bakat Palmok Chookyo Makgi
Blocking Tool: Outer Forearm

N

L

Step forward with your right foot to form a right walking stance towards N. Execute a rising block with your right outer forearm.

Walking Stance Outer Forearm Rising Block

Gunnun Sogi Bakat Palmok Chookyo Makgi

Blocking Tool: Outer Forearm

N

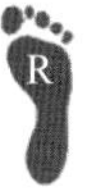

18

Pivot anti clockwise on your right foot and step across with your left foot to form a right L stance towards E. Execute a middle knife hand strike with your left hand.

L Stance Knife Hand Middle Strike
Niunja Sogi Sonkal Kaunde Taerigi
Strike Tool: Knife Hand
Target Area: Solar Plexus

L

E

Step forward with your right foot to form a right walking stance towards E. Execute a high obverse punch with your right fist.

19

Walking Stance High Obverse Punch
Gunnun Sogi Nopunde Baro Jirugi
Strike Tool: Fore Fist
Target Area: Nose

L

E

20

Pivot clockwise on your left foot and step across with your right foot to form a left L stance towards W. Execute a middle knife hand strike with your right hand.

L Stance Knife Hand Middle Strike
Niunja Sogi Sonkal Kaunde Taerigi
Strike Tool: Knife Hand
Target Area: Solar Plexus

R

W

L

Step forward with your left foot to form a left walking stance towards W. Execute a high obverse punch with your left fist. Kihap to finish.

21

Walking Stance High Obverse Punch
Gunnun Sogi Nopunde Baro Jirugi
Strike Tool: Fore Fist
Target Area: Nose

R

W

End

Pivot anti clockwise on your right foot and step across with your left foot to form a parallel ready stance towards S.

Parallel Ready Stance
Narani Junbi Sogi

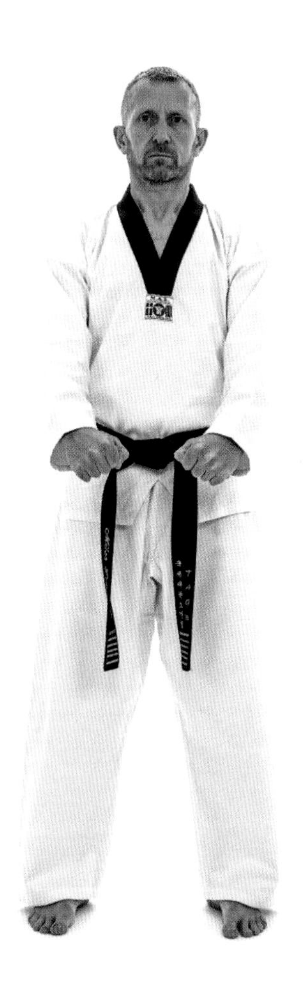

S

New Techniques

Knife Hand Middle Guarding Block
Sonkal Kaunde Daebi Makgi

Chamber Position

The half facing position allows you to protect your body from attack. Your front arm is bent at approximately 90 degrees with the fingertips level with your shoulder. Your rear hand is placed in front your chest approximately 3cm away from your body. The blocking tool reaches the target in a straight line from the chamber position, your hands rotate to generate power.

New Techniques

Twin Outer Forearm Block
Sang Bakat Palmok Makgi

Chamber Position

Twin outer forearm block combines a forearm guarding block and outer forearm rising block to allow defence from two simultaneous attacks. The chamber position for this block is achieved by crossing both arms across your chest, with the arm that will perform the upper block on the outside. Both arms reach their focus points at the same time and your upper arm should be angled at approximately 45 degrees to deflect the attacking tool away from your head.

Application of Techniques

n this example the twin outer forearm block is shown defending against two
multaneous attacks.

New Techniques

Outer Forearm Rising Block
Bakat Palmok Chookyo Makgi

Chamber Position

Ensure your fist is higher than your elbow to deflect the attack away from your head

Application of Techniques

In this example the defence is used against an attack from a pole/stick.

New Techniques

Knife Hand Middle Strike
Sonkal Kaunde Taerigi

Chamber Position

Knife hand strike is used to strike the solar plexus, throat or neck. The chamber position for this strike begins with your striking arm on the inside of your reaction arm, with your palm facing towards you. As the strike is executed your hand rotates to generate power.

In this example the strike is aimed towards the chest.

Parallel Ready Stance

1

L Stance
Knife Hand Middle
Guarding Block

4

Walking Stance
High Obverse Punch

5

Walking Stance
Outer Forearm
Low Block

2

Walking Stance
High Obverse Punch

3

L Stance
Knife Hand Middle
Guarding Block

6

Walking Stance
High Obverse Punch

7

Walking Stance
High Obverse Punch

8

Walking Stance
High Obverse Punch

9

L Stance
Twin Outer
Forearm Block

12

Walking Stance
High Obverse Punch

13

Walking Stance
Outer Forearm
Low Block

10

Walking Stance
High Obverse Punch

11

L Stance
Twin Outer
Forearm Block

14

Walking Stance
Outer Forearm
Rising Block

15

Walking Stance
Outer Forearm
Rising Block

16

Walking Stance
Outer Forearm
Rising Block

17

Walking Stance
Outer Forearm
Rising Block

20

L Stance
Knife Hand
Middle Strike

21

Walking Stance
High Obverse Punch

18

L Stance
Knife Hand
Middle Strike

19

Walking Stance
High Obverse Punch

End

Parallel Ready Stance

The Meaning of Do San

Do San is the pseudonym of the patriot Ahn Chang Ho (1876 to 1938) who devoted his life to furthering the education of Korea and its independence movement.

This pattern has 24 moves.

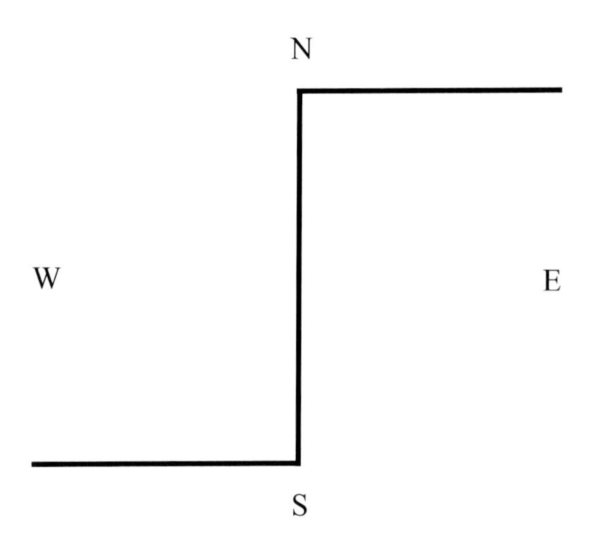

Movement Plan

Do San

Do San was born on 9th November 1878, the third son of a farmer in the South Pyeongan Province. At the age of 19 he became involved with the activities of the Korean Independence Association, but felt education rather than political protest would be a better use of his time.

Prior to the Japanese occupation (1903 to 1945) he fled to America to continue his studies and become an educator. He founded the Korean Fellowship Society to unite displaced Koreans in the USA. The unity he saw in America led him to return to Korea in 1907 and form the Sinminhoe or New People's Society which led to the formation of the Daesung School which promoted the empowering of Koreans and began the movement towards independence. This displeased the Japanese and he was exiled back to the United States in 1910.

This did not prevent Do San from continuing his fight for Korean independence and he took part in the March First Independence Movement in China in 1919. While in China he formed the Korean Independence Party.

Following unrest in Shanghai in 1932 Do San and other Korean activists were arrested and sent back to Seoul and sentenced to four years in prison, although he was released after two.

He continued to live in Korea and further the movement until again he was arrested, but due to severe illness he was released from prison and sadly passed away shortly after on the 10th March 1938.

Do San's son, Philip Ahn remained in America where he starred in several films and the TV series "Kung Fu" with David Carridine.

Ahn Chang Ho

Begin in a parallel ready stance towards S.

Parallel Ready Stance
Narani Junbi Sogi

S

Pivot anti clockwise on your right foot and step forward with your left foot to form a left walking stance towards E. Execute a high block with your left outer forearm.

1

Walking Stance Outer Forearm High Block
Gunnun Sogi Bakat Palmok Nopunde Makgi
Blocking Tool: Outer Forearm

L

E

Do San Tul

Remain in a left walking stance towards E. Execute a middle reverse punch with your right fist.

2

Walking Stance Middle Reverse Punch
Gunnun Sogi Kaunde Bandae Jirugi
Strike Tool: Fore Fist
Target Area: Solar Plexus

E

Step across with your left foot towards S. Pivot clockwise on your left foot and step across with your right foot to form a right walking stance towards W. Execute a high block with your right outer forearm.

3

Walking Stance Outer Forearm High Block
Gunnun Sogi Bakat Palmok Nopunde Makgi
Blocking Tool: Outer Forearm

R

W

L

S

4

Remain in a right walking stance towards W. Execute a middle reverse punch with your left fist.

Walking Stance Middle Reverse Punch
Gunnun Sogi Kaunde Bandae Jirugi
Strike Tool: Fore Fist
Target Area: Solar Plexus

R

W

Step across with your left foot to form a right L stance towards S. Execute a middle knife hand guarding block.

5

L Stance Knife Hand Middle Guarding Block
Niunja Sogi Sonkal Kaunde Daebi Makgi
Blocking Tool: Knife Hand

R

L

S

6

Step forward with your right foot to form a right walking stance towards S. Execute a middle straight fingertip thrust with your right fingertips.

Walking Stance Straight Fingertip Middle Thrust
Gunnun Sogi Son Sonkut Kaunde Tulgi
Strike Tool: Fingertips
Target Area: Solar Plexus

L

S

Thrust your right hand downward and twist as if to release from a grab. Your right foot moves across slightly to increase your power with a hip twist.

Release Move
Jap Yasol Tae

7

Continue to pivot anti clockwise on your right foot 360 degrees. Step forward with your left foot to form a left walking stance towards S. Execute a high side strike with your left back fist.

Walking Stance Back Fist High Side Strike
Gunnun Sogi Dung Joomuk Nopunde Yop Taerigi
Strike Tool: Back Fist
Target Area: Temple

S

Step forward with your right foot to form a right walking stance towards S. Execute a high side strike with your right back fist.

Walking Stance Back Fist High Side Strike

Gunnun Sogi Dung Joomuk Nopunde Yop Taerigi

Strike Tool: Back Fist

Target Area: Temple

L

S

9

Pivot anti clockwise on your right foot and step across with your left foot to form a left walking stance towards W. Execute a high block with your left outer forearm.

Walking Stance Outer Forearm High Block
Gunnun Sogi Bakat Palmok Nopunde Makgi
Blocking Tool: Outer Forearm

Remain in a left walking stance towards W. Execute a middle reverse punch with your right fist.

10

Walking Stance Middle Reverse Punch
Gunnun Sogi Kaunde Bandae Jirugi
Strike Tool: Fore Fist
Target Area: Solar Plexus

R

W

11

Step across with your left foot towards N. Pivot clockwise and step across with your right foot to form a right walking stance towards E. Execute a high block with your right outer forearm.

Walking Stance Outer Forearm High Block
Gunnun Sogi Bakat Palmok Nopunde Makgi
Blocking Tool: Outer Forearm

N

E

Remain in a right walking stance toward E. Execute a middle reverse punch with your left fist.

12

Walking Stance Middle Reverse Punch
Gunnun Sogi Kaunde Bandae Jirugi
Strike Tool: Fore Fist
Target Area: Solar Plexus

L

E

13

Draw your left foot backward and pivot anti clockwise on your right foot. Step forward with your left foot to form a left walking stance towards NW. Execute a high outer forearm wedging block.

Walking Stance Outer Forearm High Wedging Block
Gunnun Sogi Bakat Palmok Nopunde Hechyo Makgi
Blocking Tool: Outer Forearms

NW

Maintain the position of your arms as in move 13. Execute a middle front kick with your right foot towards NW.

14

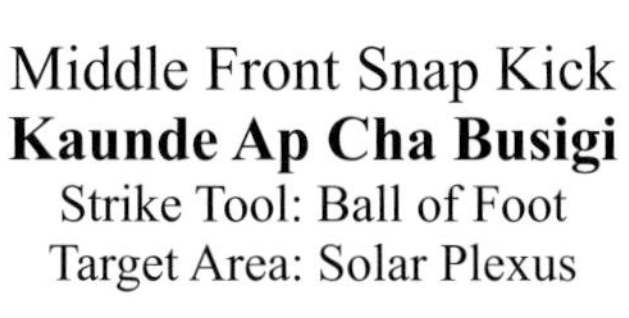
Middle Front Snap Kick
Kaunde Ap Cha Busigi
Strike Tool: Ball of Foot
Target Area: Solar Plexus

NW

15

Lower your right foot to form a right walking stance towards NW. Execute a middle obverse punch with your right fist.

Walking Stance Middle Obverse Punch
Gunnun Sogi Kaunde Baro Jirugi
Strike Tool: Fore Fist
Target Area: Solar Plexus

NW

Remain in a right walking stance towards NW. Execute a middle reverse punch with your left fist.

16

Walking Stance Middle Reverse Punch
Gunnun Sogi Kaunde Bandae Jirugi
Strike Tool: Fore Fist
Target Area: Solar Plexus

NW

17

Pivot clockwise on your left foot and step across with your right foot to form a right walking stance towards NE. Execute a high outer forearm wedging block.

Walking Stance Outer Forearm High Wedging Block
Gunnun Sogi Bakat Palmok Nopunde Hechyo Makgi
Blocking Tool: Outer Forearms

NE

Do San Tul

Maintain the position of your arms as in move 17. Execute a middle front kick with your left foot towards NE.

18

Middle Front Snap Kick
Kaunde Ap Cha Busigi
Strike Tool: Ball of Foot
Target Area: Solar Plexus

NE

19

Lower your left foot to form a left walking stance towards NE. Execute a middle obverse punch with your left fist.

Walking Stance Middle Obverse Punch
Gunnun Sogi Kaunde Baro Jirugi
Strike Tool: Fore Fist
Target Area: Solar Plexus

NE

Remain in a left walking stance towards NE. Execute a middle reverse punch with your right fist.

20

Walking Stance Middle Reverse Punch
Gunnun Sogi Kaunde Bandae Jirugi
Strike Tool: Fore Fist
Target Area: Solar Plexus

21

Pivot anti clockwise on your right foot and step across with your left foot to form a left walking stance towards N. Execute a rising block with your left outer forearm.

Walking Stance Outer Forearm Rising Block
Gunnun Sogi Bakat Palmok Chookyo Makgi
Blocking Tool: Outer Forearm

N

Step forward with your right foot to form a right walking stance towards N. Execute a rising block with your right outer forearm.

22

Walking Stance Outer Forearm Rising Block
Gunnun Sogi Bakat Palmok Chookyo Makgi
Blocking Tool: Outer Forearm

N

23

Pivot anti clockwise on your right foot and step across with your left foot to form a sitting stance towards S. Execute a knife hand strike with your left hand towards E.

Sitting Stance Knife Hand Middle Strike
Annun Sogi Sonkal Kaunde Taerigi
Strike Tool: Knife Hand
Target Area: Solar Plexus

24

Step across with your left foot placing it beside your right foot. Step your right foot across to form a sitting stance towards S. Execute a middle knife hand strike with your right hand towards W. Kihap to finish.

Sitting Stance Knife Hand Middle Strike
Annun Sogi Sonkal Kaunde Taerigi
Strike Tool: Knife Hand
Target Area: Solar Plexus

W 

L

S

End

Step across with your right foot towards E to form a parallel ready stance towards S.

Parallel Ready Stance
Narani Junbi Sogi

E

S

New Techniques

Sitting Stance
Annun Sogi

Weight Distribution
Left 50%
Right 50%

1½ Shoulder Widths

Sitting stance is 1½ shoulder widths between the big toes.
This is a training stance used to strengthen the leg muscles used in Tae Kwon Do.

New Techniques

Outer Forearm High Block
Bakat Palmok Nopunde Makgi

The chamber position requires your blocking arm to be on the inside of your reaction arm with the back of your forearms facing each other.

Middle Reverse Punch
Kaunde Bandae Jirugi

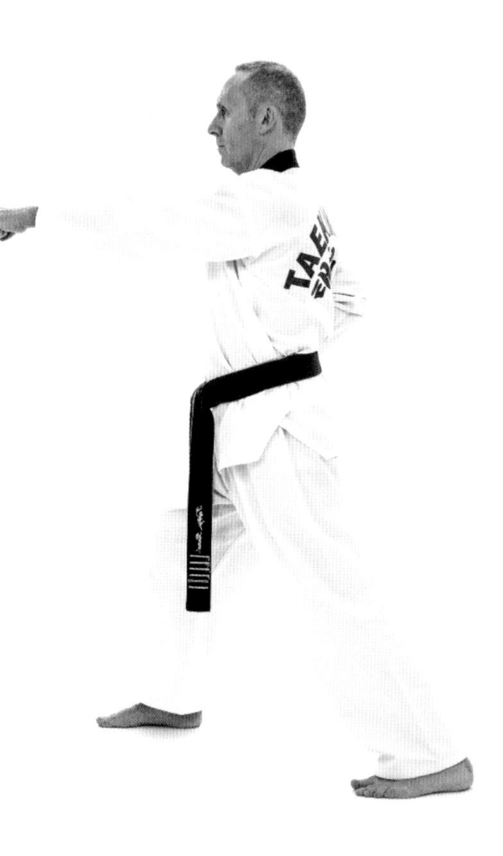

Reverse literally means the opposit arm and leg are forward.

New Techniques

Middle Front Snap Kick
Kaunde Ap Cha Busigi

The ball of your foot is used as the strike tool. The kick generates power using a combination of your hip and knee.

New Techniques

Straight Fingertip Middle Thrust
Son Sonkut Kaunde Tulgi

Chamber Position

Final Hand Position

Your lower arm acts as a block, guard and reaction. Your thrusting arm hits th target in a straight line, it does not "chop" downwards.

Application of Techniques

In this example the straight fingertip thrust is directed to the solar plexus.

New Techniques

Release Move
Jap Yasol Tae

Release move is used to break the grip of an opponent. The release is achieved by sharply twisting and thrusting the arm away breaking your attackers grip. Hip twist and shifting your front foot across increases the effectiveness of this technique.

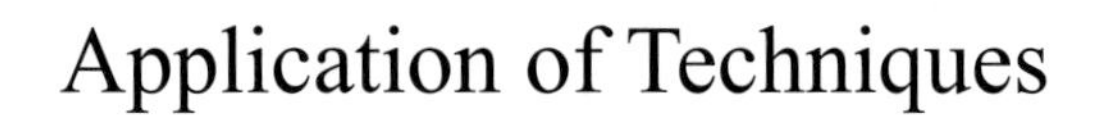

Application of Techniques

Your opponent grabs your wrist.

Sharply twist and thrust away to break your attackers grip.

New Techniques

Back Fist High Side Strike
Dung Joomuk Nopunde Yop Taerigi

Chamber Position

Back fist high side strike is used to attack either the temple or face. The chamber position is the same as an inner forearm middle block with your striking arm belo your reaction arm. The focus point is leve with your shoulder.

Application of Techniques

In this example the back fist high side strike is used to target your opponents temple.

New Techniques

Outer Forearm High Wedging Block
Bakat Palmok Nopunde Hechyo Makgi

Wedging block is used to deflect two attacks simultaneously, for example a twin vertical punch or a grab to your head. Your arms drive up between the attacking tools and then break apart to deflect the attack. Ensure that you do not open your arms beyond your own shoulder width.

Application of Techniques

his example the wedging
ck is used to prevent an
cker using a twin vertical
ch.

Do San Tul

Parallel Ready Stance

Walking Stance
Outer Forearm
High Block

Walking Stance
Middle Reverse Punch

Walking Stance
Straight Fingertip
Middle Thrust

Release Move

Walking Stance
Back Fist
High Side Strike

3

Walking Stance
Outer Forearm
High Block

4

Walking Stance
Middle Reverse Punch

5

L Stance
Knife Hand Middle
Guarding Block

8

Walking Stance
Back Fist
High Side Strike

9

Walking Stance
Outer Forearm
High Block

10

Walking Stance
Middle Reverse Punch

11

Walking Stance
Outer Forearm
High Block

12

Walking Stance
Middle Reverse Punch

15

Walking Stance
Middle Obverse Punch

16

Walking Stance
Middle Reverse Punch

17

Walking Stance
Outer Forearm
High Wedging Block

13

Walking Stance
Outer Forearm
High Wedging Block

14

Middle Front
Snap Kick

18

Middle Front
Snap Kick

19

Walking Stance
Middle Obverse Punch

20

Walking Stance
Middle Reverse Punch

21

Walking Stance
Outer Forearm
Rising Block

24

Sitting Stance
Knife Hand
Middle Strike

End

Parallel Ready Stance

Walking Stance
Outer Forearm
Rising Block

Sitting Stance
Knife Hand
Middle Strike

Index - English

Index - Korean

This page is left intentionally blank

Other books in the series

Green Belt to Blue Belt
Won Hyo
Yul Gok
Joong Gun

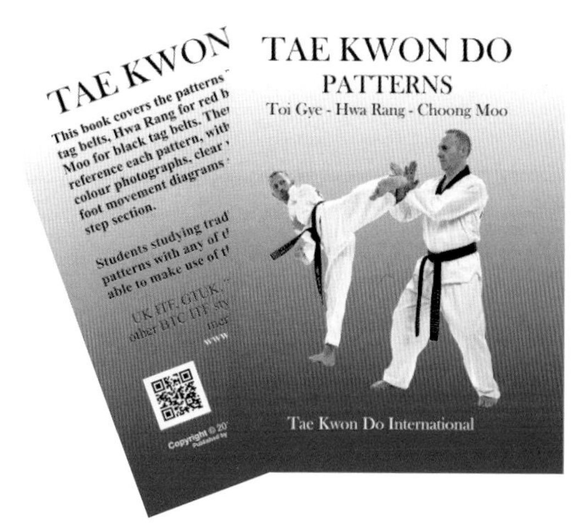

Red Tag Belt to Black Belt
Toi Gye
Hwa Rang
Choong Moo

Available via
www.tkdpromotions.com

Visit www.taekwondo-books.com

This page is left intentionally blank

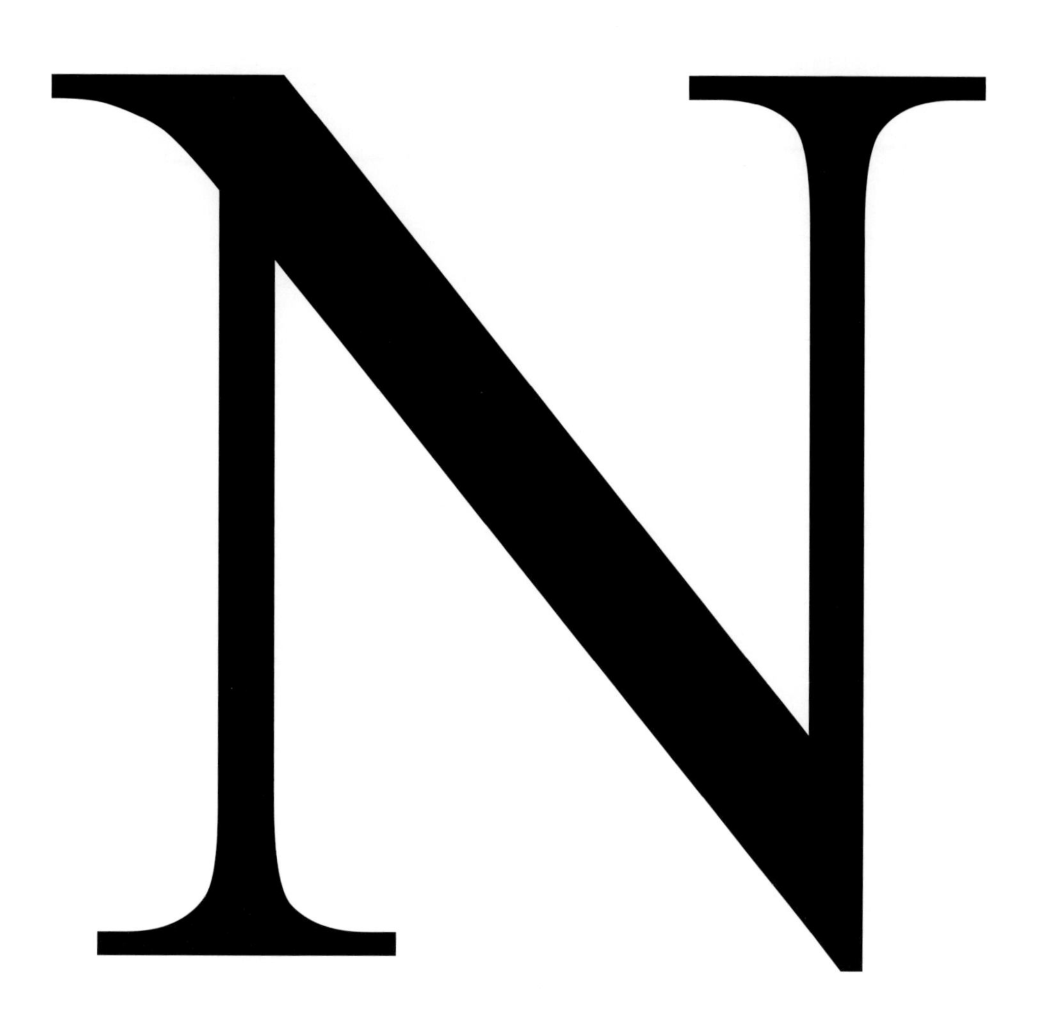

This page is left intentionally blank

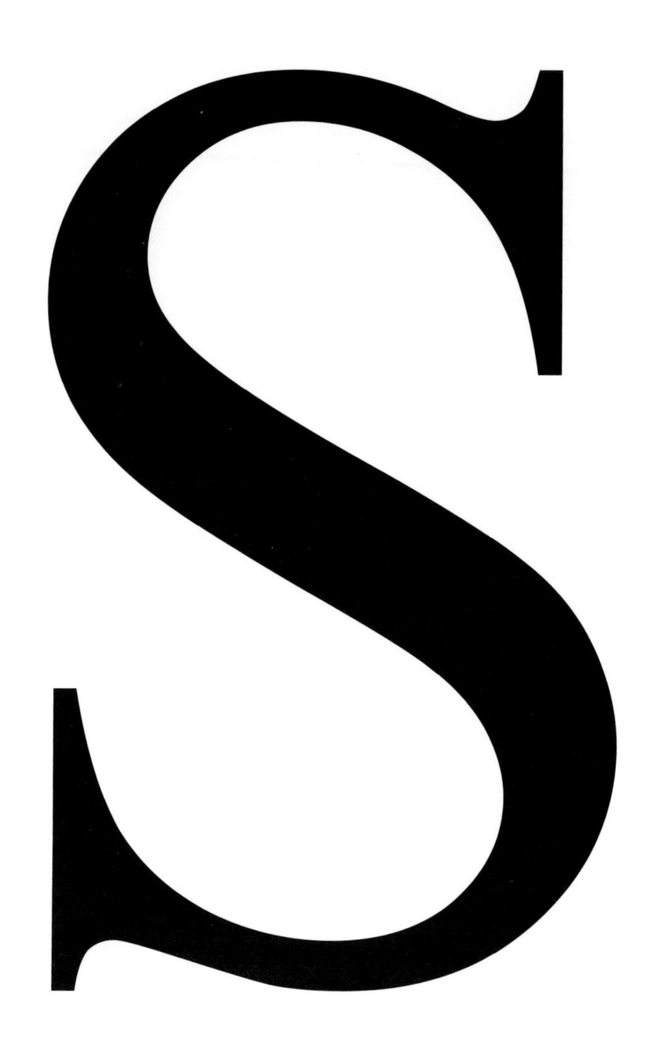

This page is left intentionally blank

This page is left intentionally blank

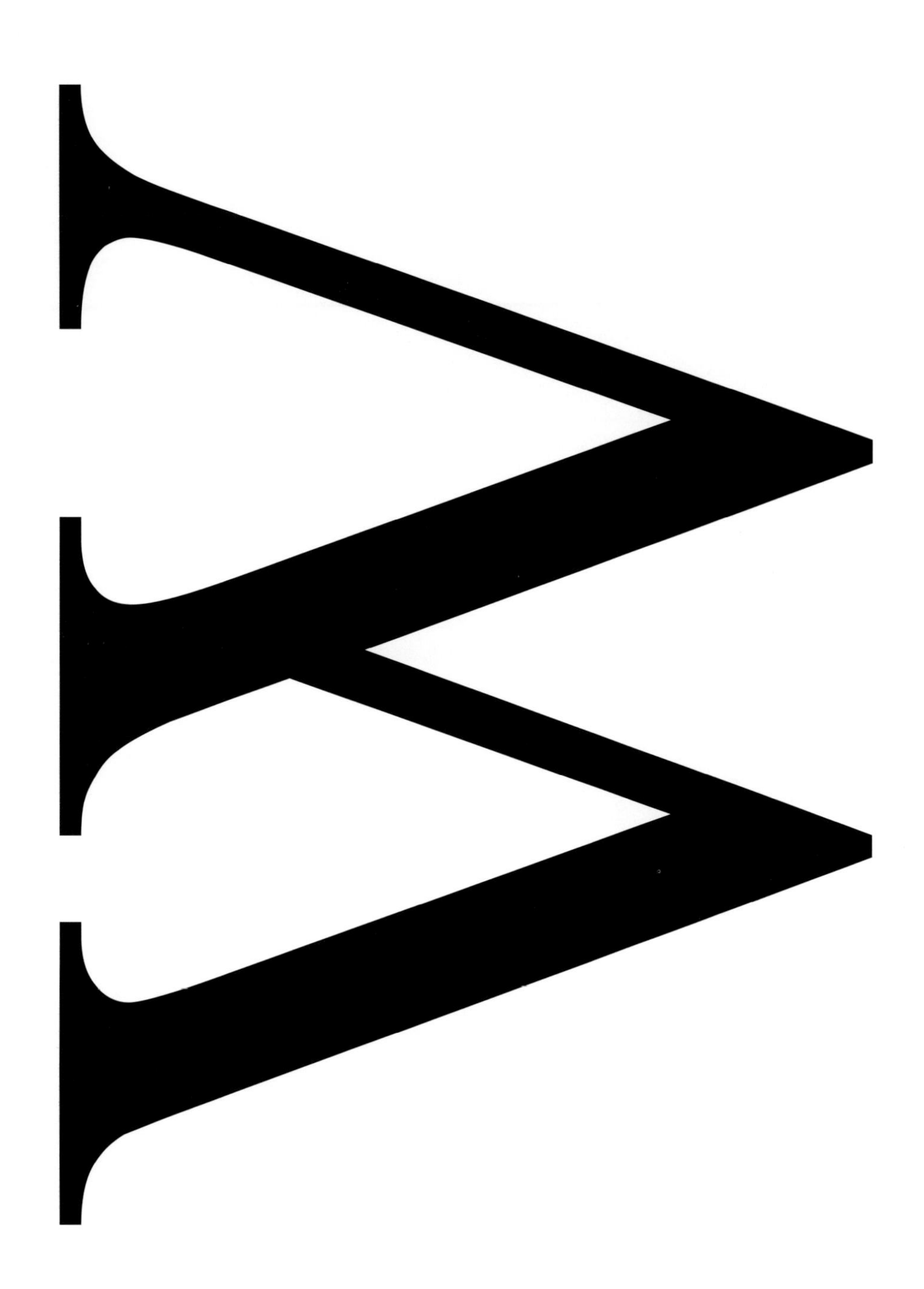

This page is left intentionally blank

This page is left intentionally blank

This page is left intentionally blank